THE BOOK OF
Finger Food

THE BOOK OF
Finger Food

HILAIRE WALDEN

PHOTOGRAPHED BY
PATRICK McLEAVEY

PUBLISHED BY
SALAMANDER BOOKS LIMITED
LONDON

Published by Salamander Books Limited
8 Blenheim Court, Brewery Road, London N7 9NT

9 8 7 6 5 4 3 2 1

© Salamander Books Ltd., 1999

ISBN 1 84065 063 X

Project managed by: Charlotte Davies
Editor: Madeline Weston
Designer: Mark Holt
Photographer: Patrick McLeavey
Photographer's Assistant: Andi Barker
Home Economist: Alison Austin
Filmset by: SX Composing Ltd, England
Reproduction: Studio Tec, England
Printed in Spain

Notes
All spoon measurements are level
1 teaspoon = 5ml spoon
1 tablespoon = 15ml spoon

CONTENTS

FOREWORD

The Book of Finger Food contains an imaginative selection of eclectic dishes for food that can be eaten easily in the fingers, in just one or two bites. The recipes are less complicated and intimidating than canapes, and more straightforward with extra emphasis being placed on flavour and overall eating enjoyment. No special skills are required, with many of the dishes being ready to eat in a short time. The recipes are based on cuisines from around the world, sometimes in new guises.

The majority of the recipes in *The Book of Finger Food* are ideal for today's casual entertaining, but there are also recipes for more formal, elegant affairs. And there are dishes to suit all tastes.

The introduction offers invaluable advice and helpful tips for planning parties, choosing dishes, creative presentation, sleek serving, and organization of drinks, all of which contribute to successful, relaxed occasions for both guests and hosts. However, the recipes in *The Book of Finger Food* are not just for parties. They also make tasty first courses, picnic fare and packed meal choices. A selection of the recipes can provide a light meal, accompanied by a salad, or form part of a buffet.

INTRODUCTION

A party should be enjoyable and relaxed for the host as well as the guests. The only way that this can happen, unless the event is an impromptu affair, is by forward thinking and planning and by making lists and a detailed time plan. Begin by deciding on the date, the type of occasion, the budget, and the number of guests. Then settle down to the vital practical and organizational aspects.

CHOICE OF FOOD
Time spent on the careful selection of the food to be served will pay dividends later both in terms of the enjoyment of the food and the calmness and confidence of the host. It will allow the host to spend time with the guests rather than being confined to the kitchen.

Consider the colours, textures and flavours of the food that

you intend to offer and try to provide contrasts, such as in texture – some crisp dishes, some soft, some smooth and some coarse. Avoid having too many similar flavours, such as a menu of all spicy dishes like Mexican, Indian and Thai. Combine light and more substantial items, and include a mixture of ingredients – meat, fish, vegetables, cheese and egg, plus some plain items, as well as one or two varieties that can be placed around the room for people to 'nibble' at, such as Savoury Palmiers. Try not to repeat the ingredients, by serving two chicken dishes for example. For the guests' convenience, and to keep the floor clean, it should be possible to eat all the items in one or two bites.

Do not be too ambitious; it is far better to keep the food simple than to attempt dishes that are overly complicated or that you do not feel at ease preparing. If you want to serve recipes that you have not tried before, make them at least once in advance. Allow enoughtime to do all

the shopping so that there is not too much to buy close to the event.

Think about how you will cook, store and heat the food. Serve a balance of hot and cold dishes and plan to have some dishes that need to be grilled, some fried and others that can be cooked in the oven. It is a good idea to start with a cold recipe that can be put out on plates before the guests arrive.

Choose a high proportion of items that can be fully or at least partly prepared, preferably frozen, in advance and keep to the minimum recipes that require last-minute attention.

PLANNING

When working out cooking times, remember that ovens are less efficient when laden, and that large pans will take longer to heat up than normal family-sized pans. Assess your equipment and utensils. Make sure that you have enough pots and pans and that they are large enough for the quantities that you will be making; borrow some if necessary, but do make sure that they will fit into the oven.

Fridge space will be at a premium with prepared items, ingredients, wines and soft drinks all requiring to be kept cool. Ask friends to lend a shelf or two in their fridges, or buy some cool boxes and ice blocks.

Bear in mind what help, if any, there will be in the kitchen both in advance and during the occasion; call on friends or family to ease the load. Also, remember to arrange for help taking the food and drink around,

choosing people who can be relied upon to keep circulating and not linger over conversations.

Provide plenty of serving plates that are large enough that they do not have to be returned to the kitchen frequently for replenishing, but not so large that the food begins to look messy. When choosing large plates, consider their weight when loaded with food, bearing in mind that someone will have to hold them for a while.

Have a plentiful supply of foil or large paper napkins for covering serving trays. Place cocktail sticks in convenient places around the room (with dishes to hold used sticks) and plenty of good quality cocktail-size paper napkins. In the kitchen you need to stock up with rubbish sacks, kitchen paper and tea towels.

Think about how and where the dishes for serving hot food will be warmed. If the oven is full, plates and dishes can be put to warm over a saucepan of water, bowl or sink of hot water (don't forget to wipe the bottom of the plate or dish before using). An electric heated trolley or hot tray will, obviously, do the job well.

Schedule time into the preparations for arranging the room, clearing and cleaning up the kitchen and, most importantly, ample time for getting yourself ready and relaxing before the guests arrive.

QUANTITIES

A variety of factors affect the quantities that will be needed, such as the time of day, the time of year, the type of occasion, who is coming, how many guests there will be (the more there are the less they will eat proportionately), and their appetites. For a finger food party, offer at least six varieties, and allow eight to ten items per person. For pre-supper eats, allow about five items per person.

PREPARATION

Empty the waste bin, clear as much work surface as possible and keep surfaces clean and free of clutter while working. Assemble all the ingredients and equipment that will be needed before starting and work on the conveyor-belt principle. For example, when preparing Prawn Toasts, prepare as much of the prawn mixture that will be needed, lay out all the slices of bread, spread with the topping, sprinkle over the sesame seeds then cut all the slices into triangles.

PRESENTATION

Appearances do matter, even if the food is given only a glance before being eaten. Plain plates show off food better and look cleaner than decorative, patterned ones. Food will be cramped on small plates, so opt for those that are larger, but not king-size. For extra impact, look for varied shapes; secondhand shops or car boot sales can unearth interesting finds. Unusual surfaces and containers look effective – mirrors, shiny black plates, foil-covered trays or other flat surfaces, and biscuit tin lids, pieces of metal with any rough edges carefully covered with sticky tape, wooden trays, a bread board or cheese board, wicker baskets, and a hollowed-out flat loaf can all be eye-catching.

For convenience and speed when it comes to adding garnishes, keep them simple, relevant and edible, and prepare them in advance of the party. A fussy, complicated garnish can soon lose its appeal when the plates are handed round and the food is removed. A sprinkling of finely chopped fresh herbs or some small herb sprigs can be added easily at the last minute and they are often all that is needed.

SERVING

Keep cold food covered until the last minute so that it looks fresh. Offer only a couple of varieties at a time, and ensure a steady flow of dishes out of the kitchen in tune with the rate at which they are being eaten.

DRINKS

Many off-licences sell wine on a sale-or-return basis and they also hire out glasses. Offer a choice of wine but keep the choice limited. Often just one red wine and one dry white wine is enough but you may like to offer a medium sweet wine as well, and some beer. Don't just offer orange juice as a non-alcoholic alternative; make a non-alcoholic punch instead.

One bottle of wine should provide 5-6 glasses, a litre bottle gives 6-8 glasses but the size of the glasses are a factor. Allow at least half a bottle per head.

To chill wine, line plastic tubs with plastic sacks and fill with ice and water. Keep in a cool place. Ice can be bought in supermarkets and off-licences – a 12.6kg (28lb) bag should chill a case of wine in about 1 hour. Move chilled bottles to the top as you put more in, or transfer them to cool boxes or bags. Wine can be opened ahead of time and the corks pressed gently back in.

STUFFED FRESH DATES

20 fresh dates
115g (4oz/½ cup) soft (cream) cheese
25g (1oz/¼ cup) pistachio nuts, finely chopped
1 tablespoon chopped stem ginger
1 tablespoon chopped fresh mint
salt and freshly ground black pepper
small mint leaves, to garnish

With point of a small, sharp knife, cut a slit along length of each date. Ease out the pits.

In a bowl, mix together remaining ingredients, except garnish. Fill dates with a little cheese mixture. Chill for 1 hour. Garnish with mint leaves and serve.

Makes 20

STUFFED CELERY

4 large sticks celery, cut diagonally into 5 pieces
celery leaves, to garnish
FILLING
50g (2oz/½ cup) pine nuts
50g (2oz) coriander (cilantro) leaves
1 plump clove garlic, crushed
50g (2oz/½ cup) freshly grated Parmesan cheese
2 tablespoons olive oil
freshly ground black pepper

To make filling, preheat grill (broiler). Spread pine nuts on a baking sheet and toast lightly, stirring frequently. Leave to cool then chop finely. With a pestle and mortar, crush toasted nuts, coriander (cilantro) and garlic together to a nubbly texture. Work in Parmesan then oil. Season to taste with pepper.

Divide filling among celery pieces. Garnish with celery leaves and serve.

Makes 20

— CAMEMBERT BAKED IN A BOX —

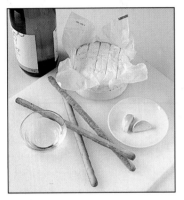

1 whole ripe but reasonably firm
  Camembert, in a box
1 clove garlic, halved
a little fruity white wine
grissini and/or crudités, to serve

Preheat oven to 200C (400F/Gas 6).
Remove cheese from box and discard the
wrapping. Return cheese to box. Rub cut
sides of garlic over top of cheese. With a
sharp knife, slice top off Camembert then
replace it on top of cheese.

Pierce 6 holes in top of cheese with a skewer
and trickle in a few drops of wine. Replace
lid of box. Bake cheese for 25-30 minutes, or
until hot and bubbling. Remove box lid and
top slice of cheese. Place box of cheese on a
plate and surround with grissini and/or
crudités. Serve immediately while cheese is
melted and runny.

Serves 6-8

ORIENTAL CRACKERS

½ red pepper (capsicum), deseeded and chopped
½ yellow pepper (capsicum), deseeded and chopped
2 teaspoons grated fresh root ginger
2 tablespoons toasted sesame seeds
2 tablespoons sesame oil
2 tablespoons light soy sauce
few drops of chilli (chili) sauce
40 prawn crackers

In a bowl, mix chopped peppers (capsicums), ginger, sesame seeds, sesame oil and soy sauce together. Season with chilli (chili) sauce to taste. Cover and keep cool for up to 4 hours.

Transfer pepper (capsicum) mixture to a cool serving bowl. Stand bowl on a serving plate and surround with prawn crackers.

Makes 40

SAVOURY PALMIERS

about 350g (12oz) puff pastry, thawed if frozen
4-6 tablespoons anchoiade (anchovy paste)
2 tablespoons chopped fresh basil
freshly ground black pepper
vegetable oil for greasing

On a lightly floured surface, roll out pastry to a 20x25cm (8x10in) rectangle. Chill for at least 30 minutes. Mix two-thirds of anchoiade with basil and pepper. Spread anchoiade mixture over pastry. Fold the two long sides over pastry to meet in centre. Press flat.

Spread remaining anchoiade on top. Fold in half and press down firmly. Slice thinly. Grease baking sheets, and place slices cut-side up on baking sheets. Chill for 30 minutes. Preheat oven to 220C (425F/Gas 7). Bake palmiers for 10 minutes. Turn them over and bake for a further 4-5 minutes until golden. Cool slightly on a wire rack and serve warm.

Makes about 24

──── TUNA CROSTINI ────

24 slices from thin French loaf
oil from jar of sun-dried tomatoes in oil, or
    virgin olive oil for brushing
200g (7oz) can tuna in brine, drained
2 tablespoons lemon mayonnaise
4 sun-dried tomatoes in oil, drained and finely
    chopped
2 tablespoons chopped fresh basil
2 tablespoons chopped fresh flat-leaf parsley
squeeze of lemon juice, to taste
salt and freshly ground black pepper
TO GARNISH
coarsely chopped capers
sliced black olives

Preheat oven to 180C (350F/Gas 4). Brush
both sides of bread with oil. Place slices on a
baking sheet and bake for about 10 minutes
until pale golden brown. Cool on a wire
rack.

In a bowl, mix together tuna, mayonnaise,
sun-dried tomatoes, basil and parsley. Add
lemon juice, and salt and pepper to taste.
Spread tuna mixture over crostini. Garnish
some of the crostini with capers and some
with black olives.

Makes 24

— CHEESE CORNMEAL SQUARES —

115g (4oz/1 cup) plain (all-purpose) flour
115g (4oz/1 cup) polenta (cornmeal)
1 tablespoon baking powder
1 tablespoon chopped fresh chives
salt and freshly ground black pepper
85g (3oz/⅓ cup) butter, melted
1 egg, beaten
150ml (5fl oz/⅔ cup) soured (sour) cream
50g (2oz/½ cup) grated Gruyère (Swiss) cheese

Preheat oven to 220C (425F/Gas 7). Grease a 20cm (8in) square cake tin (pan). In a bowl, stir together flour, polenta (cornmeal), baking powder, chives and salt and pepper. Make a well in centre. Pour in butter, egg and soured (sour) cream. Stir together to make a smooth, wet dough.

Spread dough evenly in tin (pan). Cover with cheese. Bake for 20-25 minutes until set, and golden on top. Leave to cool in tin (pan) then invert on to a chopping board. Cut into approximately 4cm (1½in) squares. Serve warm or cold, cheese-side up.

Makes about 25

—— FRUITY SAUSAGE BALLS ——

450g (1lb) good quality, well-flavoured sausages
250g (9oz/1½ cups) pitted prunes
100g (3½oz/scant 1 cup) hazelnuts, chopped
300ml (10fl oz/1¼ cups) chicken stock
100g (3½oz) redcurrant jelly
lemon juice, to taste
salt and freshly ground black pepper

Preheat oven to 180C (350F/Gas 4). Slit
sausage skins and remove meat. Chop half
prunes and mix with sausage meat and
hazelnuts. Form into 20 small balls. Place on
a baking sheet. Bake for 40 minutes.

In a blender, purée remaining prunes, the
stock and redcurrant jelly. Add lemon juice,
and salt and pepper to taste. Pour into a
small saucepan and bring just to a boil.
Transfer to a warm serving dish. Put
sausage-meat balls on a warm serving plate
and stand dish of sauce in centre.

Makes 20

── CHEESE & TOMATO KEBABS ──

225g (8oz) pecorino cheese, cut into about
  1cm (½in) cubes
24 small cherry tomatoes
3 tablespoons extra virgin olive oil
1½ tablespoons lemon juice
1 tablespoon chopped fresh parsley
1 tablespoon chopped fresh oregano
freshly ground black pepper

Thread cheese and cherry tomatoes alternately on to cocktail sticks (toothpicks). Put in a shallow, non-metallic dish.

Whisk together olive oil, lemon juice, fresh herbs and plenty of coarsely ground black pepper. Pour over kebabs, and turn them to coat in dressing; cover and marinate in the fridge for 2 hours.

Makes 24

— HOME-DRIED PEARS & CHEESE —

2 large, ripe Comice or Williams pears, peeled,
 halved, cored and thickly sliced
350g (12oz) Stilton or other blue cheese (not Danish
 or Roquefort), rind removed, cut into bite-size
 cubes

Preheat oven to 110C (225F/Gas ¼).
Spread pears on a Swiss (jelly) roll tin
(pan). Put in oven for 4-6 hours until flesh
feels firmer when pressed and, when cut,
edges curl and are browned slightly. Cool
completely.

Cut pear slices into bite-size pieces. Spear
cocktail sticks (toothpicks) with a piece of
pear and a piece of cheese.

Makes about 36

STILTON WITH WALNUT BISCUITS

225g (8oz) Stilton without rind or other blue cheese,
  crumbled
small bunch of fresh flat-leaf parsley, finely chopped
4 sticks celery, finely chopped
freshly ground black pepper
flat-leaf parsley leaves (optional), to garnish
BISCUITS (COOKIES)
25g (1oz/¼ cup) walnut halves
115g (4oz/½ cup) unsalted butter, chopped
225g (8oz/2 cups) plain (all-purpose) flour

Using a fork, mash cheese with parsley,
celery and black pepper. Cover and chill.
To make biscuits (cookies), preheat grill
(broiler). Spread walnuts on a baking sheet
and toast lightly, stirring nuts frequently.
Leave to cool, then chop nuts. Rub butter
into flour and black pepper until mixture
resembles fine breadcrumbs. Stir in nuts.
Form into a dough with 3-4 tablespoons
water. Knead lightly on a lightly floured
surface. Cover and chill for 30 minutes.

Preheat oven to 180C (350F/Gas 4). Grease
baking sheets. On a lightly floured surface,
roll out dough until thin. Use a 4cm (1½in)
cutter to cut into rounds. Re-roll trimmings
as necessary. Transfer to baking sheets and
bake for 10-15 minutes, or until browned.
Remove to a wire rack to cool. Serve
biscuits (cookies) topped with Stilton
mixture, and garnished with parsley, if you
like.

Makes about 80

PARMESAN CRISPS

melted butter for greasing
225g (8oz) Parmesan cheese, finely grated
2 tablespoons very finely chopped fresh chives

Preheat oven to 200C (400F/Gas 6). Cover baking sheets with non-stick baking paper (parchment). Sprinkle cheese in mounds on baking sheets and flatten slightly with a fork to 5cm (2in) rounds.

Bake for 2½ minutes. Sprinkle Parmesan rounds with chives and bake for a further 30 seconds. Remove Parmesan rounds from oven. Leave for 2 minutes to become crisp. Using a metal palette knife, transfer to a wire rack to cool.

Makes about 16

CREAMY CHEESE PUFFS

25g (1oz/2 tablespoons) butter
2 cloves garlic, crushed and finely chopped
115g (4oz/½ cup) mascarpone cheese
2 teaspoons prepared English mustard
salt and freshly ground black pepper
6 tablespoons freshly grated Parmesan cheese
350g (12oz) puff pastry, thawed, if frozen
1 egg, beaten

Melt butter in a small saucepan, add garlic and cook over a medium heat until softened and golden. Leave until cooled but not set. Place mascarpone cheese in a large bowl, add the mustard, salt and pepper, and 4 tablespoons of Parmesan cheese. Strain in melted butter and beat together. On a lightly floured surface, roll out pastry to 35x22.5cm (14x9in).

Cut pastry into 4 strips lengthways; cut each strip into 6. Put a heaped teaspoonful of cheese mixture in centre of 12 pieces. Brush pastry edges with beaten egg. Put a piece of pastry on top and press edges together firmly to seal. Transfer to a baking sheet. Brush top of puffs with egg and sprinkle with remaining Parmesan. Chill for 30 minutes. Preheat oven to 220C (425F/Gas 7). Bake for 10-15 minutes, or until puffed and golden. Serve straight away.

Makes 12

CRISP RICOTTA GNOCCHI

900g (2lb) ricotta cheese
150g (5oz/1¼ cups) plain (all-purpose) flour
85g (3oz/1 cup) freshly grated Parmesan cheese
1 large egg (US extra large)
salt and freshly ground black pepper
225g (8 oz/1⅔ cups) coarse semolina

In a bowl, mash ricotta, flour, Parmesan, egg and salt and pepper together with a fork until evenly blended. Cover and chill for at least 2 hours. Shape cheese mixture into about 30 walnut-size balls and roll in semolina to coat evenly.

Preheat oven to 180C (350F/Gas 4). Bring a large saucepan of salted water to simmering point. Carefully add balls in batches. As soon as balls rise to surface, remove with a slotted spoon and put in a greased shallow baking dish. Bake for about 20 minutes, or until a thin crust forms. Serve hot or at room temperature.

Makes 30

· GOATS' CHEESE & LEEK PARCELS ·

25g (1oz/2 tablespoons) unsalted butter
225g (8oz) trimmed leeks, finely chopped
115g (4oz) goats' cheese, crumbled
50g (2oz) sun-dried tomatoes in oil, drained and
    finely chopped
freshly ground black pepper
8 sheets filo pastry, each about 30x45cm (12x18in)
melted butter for brushing
sesame seeds for sprinkling

Preheat oven to 200C (400F/Gas 6). Heat butter in a large non-stick frying pan (skillet). Add leeks and fry over a medium heat until softened. Transfer to a bowl to cool. Stir in goats' cheese, tomatoes and pepper. Place a pastry sheet, on work surface (counter). Brush lightly with melted butter. Put another sheet next to it, overlapping the long edges by about 2.5cm (1in) to make 60x45cm (24x18in) rectangle. Butter lightly. Repeat with 2 more filo sheets.

Put 1 teaspoon cheese mixture at 5cm (2in) intervals on pastry. Cover with remaining pastry, buttering as before. Press between mounds of filling with side of hand. Use a large, sharp knife to cut into small parcels. Seal edges by pressing firmly. Brush with butter, sprinkle with sesame seeds and bake for 8-10 minutes.

Makes about 48

FETA FINGERS

175g (6oz) feta cheese, crumbled
85g (3oz) chopped fresh flat-leaf parsley
50g (2oz) chopped fresh dill
freshly ground black pepper
1 package filo pastry
about 250g (9oz) melted butter for brushing
sesame seeds and/or poppy seeds for sprinkling
  (optional)

Preheat oven to 200C (400F/Gas 6). Oil a baking sheet. In a bowl, mix feta cheese, parsley, dill and pepper. Working with 1 sheet of filo at a time (keep remaining sheets covered), cut into 12.5x20cm (5x8in) strips. Place 1 strip on work surface (counter) with short end towards you. Brush with melted butter. Cover with a second strip.

Put a teaspoon of cheese mixture at bottom of strip. Fold in 0.5cm (¼in) along each side. Roll up. Transfer to baking sheet, brush with melted butter and sprinkle with sesame and/or poppy seeds, if using. Repeat with remaining cheese mixture and pastry. Bake for 10 minutes, or until crisp and golden. Serve warm.

Makes about 30

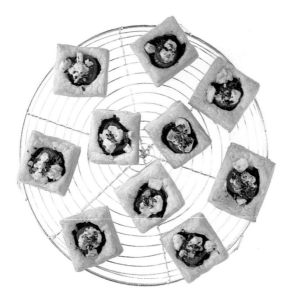

PROVENÇAL PUFFS

350g (12oz) puff pastry, thawed if frozen
2-3 tablespoons tapenade
350g (12oz) cherry tomatoes, sliced
115g (4oz) firm goats' cheese or feta cheese, chopped
freshly ground black pepper
thyme leaves, to garnish

On a lightly floured surface, roll out pastry to 35x22.5cm (14x9in). Using a large, sharp knife, cut into 4 lengthways and 8 crossways strips. Put pastry rectangles, a little apart, on 2 dampened baking sheets. Cover and chill for at least 30 minutes.

Preheat oven to 220C (425F/Gas 7). Dot a little tapenade in centre of each pastry rectangle. Put tomato slices on top then add chopped cheese. Add plenty of black pepper. Bake for 1-5 minutes or until risen and golden. Sprinkle with thyme leaves. Transfer to a wire rack. Serve warm or cold.

Makes 32

— CHEESE & WATERCRESS PUFFS —

1 bunch watercress, about 85g (3oz)
225ml (8fl oz/1 cup) milk
2 eggs, beaten
25g (1oz/2 tablespoons) butter, melted, plus extra for
  greasing
115g (4oz/1 cup) plain (all-purpose) flour
2-3 teaspoons chopped fresh parsley
salt and freshly ground black pepper
115g (4oz) fairly firm goats' cheese, cubed

Preheat oven to 220C (425F/Gas 7). Butter
about 36 mini muffin tins (pans). Put in
oven to heat. Reserve a few small watercress
sprigs for garnish. Mix remainder of
watercress with milk, eggs, butter, flour,
parsley and salt and pepper in a blender
until smooth.

Pour batter into muffin cups. Divide cheese
between cups. Bake for 15-20 minutes until
risen and golden.

Makes about 36

— ONION & CHEESE TARTLETS —

300g (10oz/2½ cups) plain (all-purpose) flour
50g (2oz/½ cup) polenta (cornmeal)
40g (1½ oz/⅓ cup) freshly grated Parmesan cheese
freshly ground black pepper
200g (7oz/generous ¾ cup) butter
3 egg yolks
450g (1lb) Spanish onions, halved and thinly sliced
300ml (10fl oz/1¼ cups) crème fraîche
115g (4oz) feta cheese, crumbled
4 whole sun-dried tomatoes, halved and thinly sliced
8 oil-cured pitted black olives, halved and
  thinly sliced
about 60 basil leaves, to garnish

In a bowl, stir flour, polenta (cornmeal),
Parmesan and black pepper together. Rub in
175g (6oz/¾ cup) of the butter until mixture
resembles crumbs. Stir in egg yolks and
enough water to make a dough. Cover and
chill for at least 30 minutes.

Meanwhile, in a large frying pan (skillet)
heat remaining butter, add onions and fry,
stirring occasionally, until beginning to
caramelize. Pour in crème fraîche. Bring to a
boil and bubble for 15-20 minutes, or until
reduced, stirring occasionally. Cool.

On a lightly floured surface, roll out pastry until thin. Using a 5cm (2in) plain cutter, cut into rounds. Use to line mini tartlet tin (pans). Prick bases and chill for 20 minutes. Preheat oven to 200C (400F/Gas 6). Bake pastry cases for 15-20 minutes. Remove to a wire rack to cool.

Stir feta and black pepper into onion mixture. Transfer tartlet cases to baking sheets.

Fill each tartlet case with 1 teaspoon onion mixture. Add a piece of sun-dried tomato and olive. Return to oven for 10 minutes. Garnish each tartlet with a basil leaf.

Makes about 60

ARTICHOKE FRITTATA

6 artichokes preserved in oil, thinly sliced
3 cloves garlic, unpeeled
3 tablespoons oil from artichokes, or olive oil
9 large eggs (US extra large)
3 tablespoons crème fraîche or whipping (heavy) cream
salt and freshly ground black pepper
3 tablespoons chopped fresh flat-leaf parsley
about 50g (2oz/½ cup) grated Gruyère cheese, for sprinkling (optional)

Preheat grill (broiler). Spread artichoke slices and garlic on a baking sheet and cook under grill (broiler) until evenly lightly charred. Remove skin from garlic, crush cloves and chop finely. In a 30cm (12in) non-stick frying pan (skillet), heat oil. In a bowl, beat eggs with crème fraîche or cream and salt and pepper. Add artichokes, garlic and parsley.

Pour egg mixture into pan and cook very slowly for about 15 minutes until body of eggs is just set and top is liquid. Sprinkle cheese over, if using. Put pan under grill (broiler) for 1-2 minutes, or until top is set or cheese has melted. Let cool, if you like. Run a palette knife around edge of frittata to loosen it and slide frittata from pan. Cut frittata into small diamond shapes.

Makes about 60

ARNOLD BENNETT SLICES

3 eggs, separated
1 tablespoon freshly grated Parmesan cheese
1 tablespoon double (heavy) cream
freshly ground black pepper
115g (4oz) smoked (Finnan) haddock
1 teaspoon lemon juice
2 tablespoons whipping (heavy) cream, beaten
1 tomato, skinned, deseeded and chopped
cayenne (chili) pepper

Preheat oven to 190C (375F/Gas 5). Line a 20x30cm (8x12in) Swiss (jelly) roll tin (pan) with greaseproof paper (baking parchment). Stir egg yolks, Parmesan, double (heavy) cream and pepper together. Beat egg whites until stiff and carefully fold into yolk mixture. Turn mixture into tin (pan) and bake for 10-12 minutes. Allow to cool. In a small saucepan, put fish and just enough water to cover. Simmer for 10 minutes then drain well and discard skin.

Chop fish finely and mix with lemon juice. Fold into whipping (heavy) cream, with tomato and black and cayenne (chili) pepper to taste. Invert omelette on to greaseproof paper (baking parchment). Carefully remove lining paper. Cut omelette in half. Spread each half with haddock mixture, almost to edges. With help of paper, roll up like a Swiss (jelly) roll. Slice each into 10 rolls.

Makes 20

SCOTCH EGGS

150g (5oz) fresh breadcrumbs
4 tablespoons finely chopped fresh tarragon
6 tablespoons capers, coarsely chopped
300g (10oz) pitted green olives, chopped
550g (1¼lb) mild goats' cheese
salt and freshly ground black pepper
175g (6oz) ciabatta bread, made into crumbs
85g (3oz/¾ cup) chopped walnuts
8 eggs, hard-boiled
sunflower oil for deep-frying
2 tablespoons mayonnaise
2 teaspoons Worcestershire sauce
2 teaspoons sun-dried tomato paste
squeeze of lemon juice
coriander (cilantro) sprigs, to garnish

In a bowl, mix breadcrumbs, tarragon, capers, olives, goats' cheese and black pepper until thoroughly combined. In a separate bowl, stir ciabatta crumbs and walnuts together. Divide cheese mixture into 8 pieces. Mould each piece smoothly around an egg. Roll in walnut mixture. Chill, uncovered, for 30 minutes.

Heat oil in a deep-fat fryer to 190C (375F). Deep-fry eggs in batches for about 2 minutes, or until golden. Drain on paper towels. Cool. Slice eggs in half. Scoop yolks into a bowl. Add mayonnaise, Worcestershire sauce, sun-dried tomato paste, and lemon juice and salt and pepper to taste. Spoon into a piping (pastry) bag fitted with a large star nozzle (tube). Pipe filling into cavities in eggs. Garnish with coriander (cilantro) sprigs.

Makes 16

— STUFFED CHERRY TOMATOES —

30 cherry tomatoes
25g (1oz/2 tablespoons) unsalted butter
4 eggs, lightly beaten
2 tablespoons double (heavy) cream
1 tablespoon finely chopped fresh dill
1 tablespoon finely chopped green olives
3 tablespoons freshly grated pecorino or
  Parmesan cheese
salt and freshly ground black pepper
sprigs of dill, to garnish

Slice off tops of tomatoes. Using a melon baller or small teaspoon, carefully scoop out insides of tomatoes; take care not to pierce skin. (Use tops and tomato flesh in sauces or soups.) Stand tomatoes upside down on paper towels. Melt butter in a non-stick saucepan. Add eggs and stir over a low heat for 1 minutes. Add cream and cook, stirring, until only very lightly cooked. Remove from heat and stir in dill, olives and one-third of cheese. Season with salt and pepper.

Preheat grill (broiler) to high. Using a teaspoon, spoon egg mixture into tomatoes, forcing mixture in with back of the spoon. Put on a baking sheet. Sprinkle remaining cheese over tomatoes. Grill for 30 seconds. Garnish with dill sprigs. Serve warm or cold.

Makes 30

CHINESE TEA EGGS

24 quails' eggs
2 tablespoons jasmine tea leaves
2 teaspoons light soy sauce
4cm (1½in) cinnamon stick
1½ star anise
salt
ground Szechuan pepper and sea salt, to serve

Put eggs into a large saucepan. Cover with plenty of water and bring slowly to a boil. Cook for 45-60 seconds. Transfer to a colander and cool under running cold water.

Simmer tea leaves in 550ml (20fl oz/ 2½ cups) of water in a small, covered pan. Strain out leaves. Tap eggs gently with back of a spoon to crack in a crazed pattern. Put in a pan in a single layer. Add tea and remaining ingredients, except Szechuan pepper and sea salt. If necessary, add more water to cover eggs. Slowly bring to a boil, cover and simmer gently for 20 minutes.

Remove pan from heat and leave eggs in water for 6 hours or overnight. Just before serving, pour away the liquid and carefully peel eggs. Mix Szechuan pepper with an equal amount of sea salt in a small serving bowl and serve with eggs.

Makes 24

- ASPARAGUS EGGS ON BRIOCHE -

16 slim green asparagus spears
8 slices brioche
40g (1½oz/3 tablespoons) butter, melted
1 tablespoon finely chopped fresh chives
salt and freshly ground black pepper
4 large eggs (US extra large), beaten
4 tablespoons crème fraîche

Preheat oven to 220C (425F/Gas 7). Cut
5cm (2in) long tips from asparagus and
discard woody stalks. Bring a saucepan of
water to a boil. Add asparagus tips and
quickly return to a boil. Boil for 30 seconds.
Drain, refresh under running cold water and
drain again. Pat dry and set aside. Using a
5cm (2in) cutter, stamp out 2 circles from
each brioche slice. Brush with 2 tablespoons
butter. Bake for 3-4 minutes or until golden.

Heat remaining butter in a non-stick
saucepan. Beat the chives and seasoning
into eggs and pour into the pan. Stir over a
low heat for 3-4 minutes until just set.
Remove from heat and stir in crème fraîche.
Divide among brioche toasts and garnish
with asparagus tips.

Makes 16

THAI SPRING ROLLS

50g (2oz) cellophane vermicelli, soaked in warm
    water for 20 minutes
8 crisp lettuce leaves, finely shredded
450g (1lb) cooked large prawns (shrimp), peeled and
    halved across
25g (1oz) fresh mint, chopped
50g (2oz) fresh coriander (cilantro), chopped
about 1 tablespoon Thai fish sauce, to taste
1 tablespoon grated fresh root ginger
4 tablespoons lime juice
1 tablespoon sesame oil
freshly ground black pepper
20x15cm (8x6in) rice flour wrappers
coriander (cilantro) sprigs, to garnish

Drain vermicelli and use scissors to cut into
short lengths. Put into a bowl and mix with
remaining ingredients, except wrappers and
garnish. Dip 1 wrapper at a time in hot
water for 30 seconds, or until just softened.
Put a heaped tablespoon prawn (shrimp)
mixture on a wrapper slightly nearer to you
than centre.

Fold sides of wrapper over filling then roll
wrapper up tightly around filling. Repeat
with remaining filling and wrappers. Cover
and refrigerate until required. Arrange on a
large serving plate and garnish with
coriander (cilantro) sprigs.

Makes 20

DEEP-FRIED FISH BITES

3 tablespoons chopped mixed fresh herbs such as
   fennel, dill, parsley, mint
115g (4oz/1 cup) dried breadcrumbs
550g (1¼lb) skinned sole (flounder) fillets, cut into
   6x1cm (2½x½in) strips
40g (1½oz/⅓ cup) plain (all-purpose) flour
2 eggs, beaten
vegetable oil for deep-frying
SAUCE
3 tablespoons Greek-style yogurt
6 tablespoons mayonnaise
2-3 tablespoons lime juice
2 tablespoons chopped fresh coriander (cilantro) or
   parsley
1 tablespoon each chopped capers and gherkins
salt and freshly ground black pepper

To make sauce, stir yogurt, mayonnaise and
lime juice together. Add herbs, capers,
gherkins and salt and pepper. Cover and
chill.

Toss together herbs, breadcrumbs and salt
and pepper. In batches, put the fish in a
large bag, add flour and toss to coat fish in
flour. Dip fish in egg then roll in herbed
breadcrumbs. Heat oil in a deep fryer to
190C (375F). Deep-fry fish in batches for
about 2 minutes, or until golden. Drain on
paper towels. Serve warm with sauce.

Makes about 60

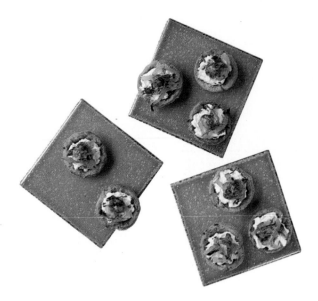

— GRAVADLAX CROUSTADES —

6 slices medium thick light rye bread, crusts removed
115g (4oz/½ cup) unsalted butter, melted
about 5 tablespoons mascarpone cheese or
   soured (sour) cream
225g (8oz) gravadlax, finely chopped
fresh dill, to garnish

Preheat oven to 180C (350F/Gas 4). Roll out each slice of bread as thinly as possible. Using a 5cm (2in) cutter, stamp out rounds. Brush rounds on both sides with melted butter then press into mini tartlet tins. Bake for 15-20 minutes, or until crisp and brown. Remove to a wire rack and cool.

Spoon mascarpone cheese or soured (sour) cream into each croustade case. Top with gravadlax then a little of the sauce that comes with gravadlax. Garnish with fresh dill.

Makes 24

—— SPINACH & PRAWN ROLLS ——

225g (8oz/1 cup) Thai jasmine (fragrant) rice
2.5cm (1in) piece fresh root ginger, grated
2 teaspoons Thai fish sauce
4 spring onions (scallions), finely chopped
225g (8oz) large spinach leaves, stalks removed
225g (8oz) peeled, cooked, large prawns (shrimp),
  chopped
salt

Put rice in a saucepan with 425ml (15fl oz/
scant 2 cups) water. Bring to a boil, cover
and cook for 10 minutes. Remove from heat
and leave to cool for 5 minutes, without
lifting lid. Remove lid. Stir in the ginger,
fish sauce and spring onions (scallions).
Leave until cold. Add spinach to a large
saucepan of boiling water for a few seconds.
Drain, rinse in cold water and drain again.
Spread leaves out in a single layer on a cloth
to dry.

Spread 4 sheets clear film (plastic wrap) on
work surface (counter). Lay spinach on top
to make 4 rectangles about 15x25cm
(6x10in), overlapping as necessary. Mix
prawns (shrimp) and salt into rice and
spread over leaves. Press down with wetted
hands. Starting from long edge, roll up
leaves tightly, enclosing filling. Wrap
tightly in clear film (plastic wrap). Chill for
at least 1 hour. Remove film (wrap) and cut
each roll into 10 slices to serve.

Makes 40

SMOKED SALMON ROLLS

225g (8oz/1 cup) full-fat soft (cream) cheese
2½-3 tablespoons finely chopped fresh chives
about 1 tablespoon lemon juice
salt and freshly ground black pepper
about 250g (9oz) sliced smoked salmon
lemon wedges (optional), to serve

Beat cheese, then beat in chives, lemon juice, a little salt and plenty of pepper. Cover and chill for at about 4 hours.

Spread cheese mixture over slices of smoked salmon and roll up tightly. Chill. Using a large, sharp knife, cut rolls into 0.5cm (¼in) slices. Arrange, cut-side up, on a cold serving platter. Add lemon wedges, if you like, and serve.

Makes about 70

SMOKED SALMON SUSHI

2 sheets toasted nori seaweed
1 teaspoon wasabi powder or horseradish cream
15g (½oz) pickled ginger
175g (6oz) sliced smoked salmon
¼ cucumber, cut into matchsticks
Japanese soy sauce for dipping
SUSHI RICE
175g (6oz/¾ cup) Japanese rice
3 tablespoons rice vinegar
2.5cm (1in) piece kelp (optional)
pinch of sugar
salt

To prepare sushi rice, put rice, vinegar, kelp, if using, and 250ml (9fl oz/1 cup plus 2 tablespoons) water in a saucepan. Cover and simmer until water has evaporated. Leave, still covered, for 10 minutes. Discard kelp, if used, and season with sugar and salt.

Lay a nori sheet on greaseproof paper (baking parchment). Spread a thin layer of rice to 3 edges but leaving 5cm (2in) clear at far edge. Sprinkle with wasabi, or spread with horseradish. Arrange line of ginger across near edge, then top with salmon slice and a few sticks of cucumber. Using greaseproof paper (baking parchment), roll up sushi to a tight cylinder. Leave to set for 1 hour. With a very sharp knife, cut into 1cm (½in) slices. Serve with a small bowl of soy sauce.

Makes about 20

MARYLAND CRAB CAKES

150g (5oz) cooked white crabmeat
85g (3oz) cooked skinless white fish such as cod or
   haddock, finely flaked
100g (3½oz) tortilla chips, finely crushed
2 tablespoons chopped fresh coriander (cilantro)
1 tablespoon ginger juice (see Note)
1 tablespoon lime juice
100g (3½oz/scant ½ cup) mayonnaise
1 tablespoon Dijon mustard
freshly ground black pepper
2 eggs, beaten
vegetable oil for frying

Mix crab, white fish, half the tortilla chips,
the coriander (cilantro), ginger and lime
juices, mayonnaise, mustard and black
pepper together. Cover and chill for at least
1 hour. With floured hands, form into
24 balls, then flatten them into cakes
(patties). Dip in beaten egg then coat in
remaining tortilla chips.

Fry cakes (patties) in hot oil in batches in a
non-stick frying pan (skillet) for 2 minutes
each side, until crisp and golden. If you like,
leave to cool. Reheat, uncovered, for
10 minutes at 200C (400F/Gas 6).

Makes 24

NOTE: To make ginger juice, grate
40g (1½oz) fresh root ginger then squeeze to
give 1 tablespoon.

— GINGER SCONES WITH CRAB —

225g (8oz/2 cups) plain (all-purpose) flour
salt and freshly ground black pepper
1½ teaspoons baking powder
1cm (½in) fresh root ginger, grated
225ml (8fl oz/1 cup) double (heavy) cream
6-7 tablespoons milk
melted butter for brushing and greasing
175g (6oz) fresh white crabmeat
2 teaspoons lemon juice
150ml (5fl oz/⅔ cup) soured (sour) cream

Preheat oven to 200C (400F/Gas 6). Grease
a baking sheet. In a bowl, stir together flour,
salt and pepper, baking powder and ginger.
Lightly work in cream and enough milk to
make a soft dough. Turn on to a lightly
floured surface and knead gently once or
twice. With finger-tips, press carefully to
1cm (½in) thick. Using a 2.5cm (1in) plain
cutter, stamp out scones (biscuits). Transfer
to baking sheet. Brush tops with melted
butter. Bake for 10 minutes, or until risen
and golden. Transfer to a wire rack to cool.

Meanwhile, in a bowl, stir together
crabmeat, lemon juice and salt and pepper.
Split scones (biscuits) in half. Add a little
soured (sour) cream to bottom halves. Top
with crab mixture, replace tops and serve.

Makes about 14

———— GOLDEN CRAB TARTS ————

1 quantity pastry (see page 30)
1 egg, beaten
3 tablespoons chopped fresh flat-leaf parsley
pinch of saffron threads, crushed
150ml (5fl oz/⅔ cup) double (heavy) cream
squeeze of lemon juice
salt and freshly ground black pepper
225g (8oz) white crabmeat, flaked
fresh flat-leaf parsley, to garnish

On a lightly floured surface, roll out pastry thinly. Stamp out about 60 rounds using a 5cm (2in) cutter. Use to line mini tartlet tins (pans). Prick bases well and chill for at least 30 minutes. Preheat oven to 200C (400F/Gas 6). Bake pastry cases for 10 minutes, or until golden. Cool on a wire rack, if you like.

Meanwhile, beat egg, parsley and saffron into cream. Season with lemon juice, and salt and pepper. Divide crabmeat among pastry cases. Spoon in some saffron cream. Return to oven for 5-10 minutes. Serve warm, garnished with parsley.

Makes about 60

PRAWN TOASTS

250g (9oz) peeled fresh prawns (shrimp)
3 spring onions (scallions), chopped
6 basil or coriander (cilantro) leaves
1 teaspoon grated fresh root ginger
small piece of orange rind
2 teaspoons cornflour (cornstarch)
½ teaspoon sesame oil
2 teaspoons rice wine or dry sherry
1 egg white
salt and freshly ground black pepper
6 slices from good quality large loaf, crusts removed
about 2 tablespoons sesame seeds
groundnut oil for frying
lime wedges, to serve

Put all ingredients except bread, sesame seeds and groundnut oil in a blender or food processor. Mix to a fairly smooth paste. Spread paste on bread and sprinkle with sesame seeds. Cut into triangles or fingers, or into crescents using a pastry (cookie) cutter.

Heat 1cm (½in) depth groundnut oil in a large frying pan (skillet) until a cube of bread browns in 40 seconds. Add bread in batches, paste side down. Fry for 1 minute then turn over and fry for 15-20 seconds until golden. Drain on paper towels. Keep warm and uncovered. Serve with lime wedges.

Makes about 24

— CURRIED PRAWNS ON NAAN —

1 tablespoon groundnut oil
4 spring onions (scallions), finely chopped
1 clove garlic, crushed
2 teaspoons fragrant curry powder
350g (12oz) cooked, peeled prawns (shrimp),
   coarsely chopped
4 teaspoons natural (plain) yogurt
4 teaspoons mango chutney
salt and freshly ground black pepper
2 large naan breads, each about 150g (5oz)
coriander (cilantro) leaves, to garnish

Heat oil in a frying pan (skillet), add spring onions (scallions) and garlic and fry for 2 minutes. Stir in curry powder and prawns (shrimp). Cook gently for 2 minutes. Remove pan from heat and stir in yogurt, chutney and salt and pepper.

Heat bread according to package instructions. Cut bread into small squares. Top with a little prawn (shrimp) mixture and garnish with coriander (cilantro) leaves.

Makes 60

— MUSSELS ON GARLIC BREAD —

20 slices from small baguette, 2.5cm (1in) thick
1 large clove garlic, halved lengthways
40g (1½oz/3 tablespoons) butter
3 shallots, finely chopped
150ml (5fl oz/⅔ cup) medium-bodied dry white wine
400g (14oz) small mussels, cleaned
2 tablespoons chopped fresh basil
large pinch of saffron threads
300ml (10fl oz/1¼ cups) double (heavy) cream
salt (if necessary) and freshly ground black pepper
fresh basil, to garnish

Preheat oven to 190C (375F/Gas 5).
Remove some of the crumb from centre of
baguette slices. Rub remaining bread with
the cut side of 1 piece of garlic. In a large
saucepan, heat butter, then add shallots and
remaining garlic. Fry for 5 minutes, until
soft. Pour in wine and bring to a boil.

Add mussels, cover and steam for 3-4
minutes, until mussels have opened. Discard
any that remain closed. Remove mussels
from shells. Strain liquid and return to
rinsed pan. Add basil, saffron and cream.
Boil until reduced to a coating consistency.
Season to taste. Return mussels to pan and
warm for 1-2 minutes over a medium heat.
Bake bread 5-8 minutes, until lightly
coloured and just crisp. Spoon mussels and
sauce on to bread slices. Garnish with basil.

Makes 20

— MEDITERRANEAN MUSSELS —

2 shallots, very finely chopped
1 clove garlic, finely crushed
4 tablespoons red pesto
freshly ground black pepper
115g (4oz/½ cup) butter, softened
85ml (3fl oz/⅓ cup) dry white wine
sprig of rosemary
2.75kg (6lb) mussels, cleaned
25g (1oz/¼ cup) freshly grated Parmesan cheese
25g (1oz) ciabatta bread, made into crumbs
finely chopped fresh parsley, to garnish

Beat shallots, garlic, red pesto and black pepper into butter. Set aside. Add wine and rosemary to a large saucepan and bring to a boil. Add mussels, cover and simmer for 3-5 minutes, or until mussels open; shake the pan occasionally. Discard any mussels that remain closed.

Preheat grill (broiler). Line a large grill (broiler) pan with crumpled foil. Remove the top shells from mussels and stand bottom shells in foil. Divide flavoured butter among mussels. Stir together Parmesan and ciabatta crumbs. Sprinkle over mussels. Grill (broil) for about 5 minutes, or until golden. Sprinkle finely chopped parsley over and serve.

Makes about 30

SEARED SCALLOP KEBABS

48 queen (bay) or small scallops
16 rosemary sprigs, or small bamboo skewers
rocket leaves, to serve
DRESSING
4 tablespoons walnut oil
2 tablespoons sherry vinegar
50g (2oz) sun-dried tomatoes in oil, chopped
leaves from 1 small bunch of basil, chopped
freshly ground black pepper

To make dressing, whisk together walnut oil and vinegar. Stir in sun-dried tomatoes and basil. Season with black pepper. Set aside.

If using bamboo skewers, soak in water for 30 minutes. Thread 3 scallops on each rosemary sprig or bamboo skewer. Place in a shallow dish, pour dressing over and turn scallops to coat in dressing. Leave in a cool place for 30 minutes. Preheat grill (broiler). Remove scallops from marinade and cook under hot grill (broiler) for about 2 minutes, turning occasionally and basting with remaining marinade. Serve on a bed of rocket leaves.

Makes 16

PINK SEAFOOD CROÛTES

50g (2oz/¼ cup) butter, melted
8 thin slices bread
FILLING
1 tablespoon butter
1 clove garlic, crushed
2 spring onions (scallions), chopped
1 tablespoon chopped fresh tarragon
150g (5oz) fresh mixed seafood cocktail
4 tablespoons lemon mayonnaise
1 tablespoon sun-dried tomato paste
freshly ground black pepper

Preheat oven to 200C (400F/Gas 6). Butter
16 small tartlet tins (pans) with some
melted butter. With a 5cm (2in) cutter,
stamp rounds from bread slices. Fit into
tartlet tins (pans), pressing in well. Brush
with remaining butter. Bake for 10-15
minutes, or until crisp and golden. Transfer
to a wire rack to cool.

To make filling, in a small pan, heat butter,
add garlic and fry until softened. In a bowl,
mix spring onions (scallions), tarragon,
seafood, mayonnaise, sun-dried tomato
paste, garlic and black pepper. Divide
among the tartlet cases.

Makes 16

———— CHICKEN BREAST ROLLS ————

4 boneless chicken breasts, skinned
85g (3oz/⅓ cup) ricotta cheese
4 tablespoons black olive tapenade
4 sun-dried tomatoes in oil, chopped
freshly ground black pepper
8 spinach leaves
150ml (5fl oz/⅔ cup) chicken stock
150ml (5fl oz/⅔ cup) medium-bodied dry white wine

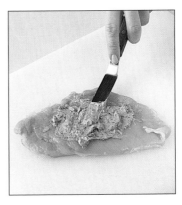

Put each chicken breast between 2 sheets of clear film (plastic wrap). Using a rolling pin, beat thinly. Remove film (wrap). Beat together ricotta, tapenade, sun-dried tomatoes and plenty of pepper. Spread over chicken.

Cover each piece of chicken with 2 spinach leaves. Roll up each breast into a thin roll. Secure with wooden cocktail sticks (toothpicks). Wrap in foil and chill for 30 minutes.

Pour stock and wine into a deep frying pan (skillet) that chicken rolls will just fit. Heat to a simmer, add foil-wrapped chicken, cover and poach for 5 minutes. Remove from heat and let chicken cool in liquid for 30 minutes. Remove and cool completely. Discard foil and cut rolls into 1cm (½in) slices. Arrange on a serving plate.

Makes 20-25

— CHICKEN & HAM WONTONS —

450g (1lb) skinless chicken fillets, chopped
115g (4oz) Parma ham, chopped
4cm (1½in) piece fresh root ginger, grated
small handful of fresh coriander (cilantro)
1 clove garlic, crushed
2 spring onions (scallions), chopped
1 egg white
freshly ground black pepper
24 rectangular wonton wrappers
groundnut oil for deep-frying

Put chicken, ham, ginger, coriander (cilantro), garlic, spring onions (scallions), egg white and black pepper in a food processor. Mix to a coarse purée so that ingredients hold together but there are discernible pieces.

Put a heaped teaspoonful of chicken mixture in centre of one wrapper. Brush edges of wrapper with water. Fold corners to centre and pinch together. Pinch along seams to seal. Put on a floured baking sheet. Repeat with remaining wrappers. Chill for up to 6 hours, wrapped in clear film (plastic wrap) if you like. Preheat a deep pan of oil to 180C (350F). Deep-fry wontons in batches for 3-4 minutes until puffed and golden. Drain on paper towels and keep warm.

Makes 24

— STICKY CHICKEN LOLLIPOPS —

15 chicken wings, about 700g (1½lb) total weight
1 teaspoon coriander seeds
¾ teaspoon cardamom seeds
5 tablespoons tomato ketchup
2 tablespoons maple syrup
1 tablespoon allspice
2 teaspoons paprika
pinch dried red chilli (chili) flakes
grated rind of 1 small lime

Cut off chicken wing tips at joint; discard.
Using a sharp knife, cut through skin and
tendons on either side of bone. Hold bone
end and scrape flesh down to other end.

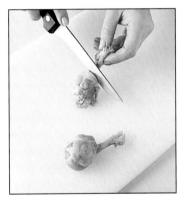

In a dry, small, heavy frying pan (skillet),
heat coriander and cardamom seeds until
fragrant. Crush in a pestle and mortar and
mix with remaining ingredients.

Place chicken pieces in a large non-stick
roasting tin (pan). Pour ketchup mixture
over chicken and turn and stir until evenly
coated. Leave to marinate in a cool place for
1 hour. Preheat the oven to 220C
(425F/Gas 7). Bake chicken for 45 minutes,
until charred and sticky, turning pieces
occasionally. Serve straight away.

Makes 15

—— MINI CHICKEN TIKKA ——

300ml (10fl oz/1¼ cups) natural (plain) yogurt
2 cloves garlic, crushed
2 teaspoons grated fresh root ginger
2 teaspoons tomato purée (paste)
grated rind and juice 1 lime
2 teaspoons garam masala
¼ teaspoon each of ground cumin, coriander and
  chilli powder (ground chilies)
salt and freshly ground black pepper
450g (1lb) chicken breast meat, cut into
  bite-size pieces
RAITA
½ cucumber, finely chopped
300ml (10fl oz/1¼ cups) Greek-style yogurt
2 tablespoons finely chopped fresh mint

In a bowl, stir together yogurt, garlic, ginger, tomato purée (paste), lime rind and juice, spices and salt and pepper. Stir in chicken, cover and refrigerate overnight.

To make raita, dry cucumber and mix with yogurt, mint and salt and pepper. Chill until required. Just before serving, preheat grill (broiler). Remove chicken from marinade and spread in a roasting tin (pan). Cook for 6-8 minutes, or until reddish-brown and cooked through. Spear with cocktail sticks (toothpicks) and serve with raita.

Makes 24

FRAGRANT CHICKEN

400g (14oz) chicken breast meat, cut into thin strips
2 cloves garlic, crushed
1 fresh red chilli (chili), deseeded and chopped
2 pinches of saffron threads
4 tablespoons olive oil
salt
handful of mint leaves
juice of 1 large lemon

Thread chicken strips on to wooden skewers. Place in a shallow non-metallic dish. Put garlic, chilli (chili), saffron, olive oil, salt and most of the mint and lemon juice in a blender. Mix to a purée. Pour over chicken, turn to coat in purée and leave to marinate for 30 minutes.

Preheat a ridged grill pan and oil lightly. Add skewers with marinade clinging to chicken strips. Cook on pan for 3-4 minutes each side, or until golden and cooked through. Mix remaining mint and lemon juice and sprinkle over chicken just before serving.

Makes about 20

— CRISP DUCK PANCAKE ROLLS —

2 duck breasts, each about 225g (8oz)
2 cloves garlic, crushed
2.5cm (1in) piece fresh root ginger, grated
2 tablespoons clear honey
2 tablespoons dry sherry
about 150ml (5fl oz/⅔ cup) Chinese plum sauce
225g (8oz/2 cups) plain (all-purpose) flour
salt and freshly ground black pepper
2 eggs, beaten
550ml (20fl oz/2½ cups) milk and water mixed
sesame oil for frying
1 cucumber, peeled, halved, deseeded and cut in
   5cm (2in) lengths
1 bunch spring onions (scallions), cut in 5cm (2in)
   long strips
3 tablespoons chopped fresh coriander (cilantro)

Slash duck breasts 3 times each with a sharp knife. In a shallow dish, mix garlic, ginger, honey and sherry, and marinate duck in a cool place for 1 hour. Preheat oven to 200C (400F/Gas 6).

Place duck on a rack over a roasting tin (pan) and roast for 15 minutes. Let cool. Remove fat and skin from duck, and spoon off fat from juices in roasting tin (pan). Stir juices left in tin (pan) into plum sauce.

Sift flour and salt and pepper into a bowl. Make a well in centre, add eggs and milk mixture and gradually draw in flour to make a smooth batter. Leave for 30 minutes. Heat and lightly oil a 15cm (6in) frying pan (skillet). Pour in a small ladleful of batter, tip and rotate pan so batter flows evenly over base. Cook for 1 minute, or until brown. Turn over and cook for 30 seconds. Remove and repeat with remaining batter to make about 12 pancakes. Leave to cool.

Slice duck then cut into thin strips. Mix with the cucumber, spring onions (scallions) and coriander (cilantro).

Cut pancakes into quarters. Spread plum sauce over each quarter. Top with a small spoonful of duck mixture. Fold pancakes tightly into rolls and secure with cocktail sticks (toothpicks).

Makes 48-60

— TURKEY & CRANBERRY ROLLS —

25g (1oz/2 tablespoons) butter
1 shallot, finely chopped
85g (3oz) fresh breadcrumbs
1 tablespoon chopped fresh flat-leaf parsley
1 tablespoon fresh thyme
1 teaspoon finely grated lemon rind
1 egg, beaten
salt and freshly ground black pepper
4x115g (4oz) turkey breast fillets
50g (2oz) cranberries, thawed if frozen
225g (8oz) thinly-sliced rindless streaky bacon

Preheat oven to 200C (400F/Gas 6). Heat butter in a frying pan (skillet) and fry shallot until soft. In a bowl, stir together breadcrumbs, shallot, parsley, thyme, lemon rind, egg and salt and pepper. Place each turkey fillet between sheets of clear film (plastic wrap) and beat with a rolling pin to flatten. Season with pepper. Spread stuffing over each turkey fillet. Arrange cranberries down length of stuffing.

Roll up each fillet from a long edge. Wrap in bacon, overlapping slices slightly. Roast for 20-25 minutes, or until bacon is crisp and turkey cooked through. Cut into 2.5cm (1in) slices. Spear with cocktail sticks (toothpicks). Serve warm or cold.

Makes 32

– PARMA-WRAPPED ASPARAGUS –

8 sheets of filo pastry
50g (2oz/¼ cup) unsalted butter, melted
50g (2oz/½ cup) freshly grated pecorino or
  Parmesan cheese
freshly ground black pepper
8 thin slices Parma ham
8 fat asparagus spears, trimmed
sesame seeds for sprinkling
lemon wedges, to serve

Preheat oven to 230C (450F/Gas 8). Lay one filo sheet on work surface (counter); keep remaining sheets covered. Brush filo sheet with melted butter and fold in half.

Sprinkle cheese and black pepper over pastry and place a slice of ham on top. Place asparagus across ham. Roll up pastry enclosing ham and asparagus.

Brush rolls with butter and sprinkle sesame seeds over. Transfer to a non-stick baking sheet. Repeat with remaining ingredients. Bake for 10 minutes until crisp and golden. Serve hot or at room temperature, with lemon wedges.

Makes about 60

MERGUEZ CRACKERS

225g (8oz) fresh spinach
50g (2oz/¼ cup) butter, melted
85g (3oz) merguez or chorizo sausage cut into
  5mm (¼in) cubes
85g (3oz/⅓ cup) ricotta cheese
salt and freshly ground black pepper
about 150g (5oz) filo pastry, cut into 7.5cm
  (3in) squares

Cook spinach in a covered pan until leaves
wilt. Drain well and squeeze out as much
water as possible. Coarsely chop and leave
to cool.

Preheat oven to 200C (400F/Gas 6). Butter
a baking sheet with a little butter. Fry
merguez or chorizo without any fat until
lightly browned. Drain on paper towels and
set aside to cool. In a bowl, mix together
spinach, merguez or chorizo and ricotta
cheese. Season to taste with salt and pepper.

Stack filo squares in pairs, buttering each
square. Put a little spinach mixture in centre
of each stack, roll up and pinch pasty ends
to resemble Christmas crackers. Place on
the baking sheet. Bake for 10-12 minutes
until crisp and golden. Serve warm.

Makes about 24

MINI 'TOAD-IN-THE-HOLE'

225g (8oz/2 cups) plain (all-purpose) flour
450ml (16fl oz/2 cups) milk
2 eggs, beaten
4 tablespoons wholegrain mustard
salt and freshly ground black pepper
4 tablespoons vegetable oil
20 good quality herbed chipolatas or other thin
  sausages

Put flour, milk, eggs, mustard and salt and
pepper in a food processor or blender and
mix until evenly combined. Leave in a cool
place for at least 30 minutes.

Preheat oven to 220C (425F/Gas 7). Lightly
brush mini muffin tins (pans) with oil. Cut
sausages into pieces that will fit in muffin
cups. Put a piece of sausage in each muffin
cup and cook in the oven for 15 minutes, or
until beginning to brown.

Working with 1 tin (pan) at a time, quickly
pour about 1 tablespoon batter over each
sausage piece and return to the oven for
15-20 minutes, or until risen and golden.
Serve warm.

Makes about 60

MOROCCAN MEATBALLS

4 tablespoons sunflower oil
1 small onion, finely chopped
1 clove garlic finely crushed
400g (14oz/1¾ cups) minced (ground) lamb
50g (2oz) fresh breadcrumbs
1 teaspoon each ground cumin, coriander and paprika
2 tablespoons each chopped fresh parsley and
   coriander (cilantro), finely chopped
2 tablespoons capers, finely chopped
1 tablespoon lemon rind
salt and freshly ground black pepper
flour for coating
paprika for sprinkling
yogurt and coriander (cilantro) dip (see page 74),
   to serve

Heat 1 tablespoon of the oil in a frying pan
(skillet). Fry onion and garlic until soft.
Cool. Pass meat through mincer (grinder)
several times. Knead in breadcrumbs, onion,
garlic, spices, herbs, capers, lemon rind and
salt and pepper. Cover and set aside for at
least 2 hours.

Preheat grill (broiler). With floured hands,
form meat mixture into about 24 small balls.
Heat remaining oil in a large frying pan
(skillet) and fry meat balls in batches,
shaking pan, for 5 minutes or until evenly
browned. Drain on paper towels. Sprinkle
with paprika and serve with dip.

Makes about 24

PORK NUGGETS

800g (1¾lb) boneless lean pork, cut into 2.5cm
 (1in) cubes
25g (1oz) coriander (cilantro) leaves
3 cloves garlic, peeled
3cm (1¼in) piece fresh root ginger, sliced
1 lemon grass stalk, outer layers removed
grated rind of 1 lime
large bunch of spring onions (scallions)
2 large fresh red chillies (chilies), deseeded
2 tablespoons soy sauce
2 tablespoons clear honey
2 tablespoons white wine vinegar
2 tablespoons Thai fish sauce
2 tablespoons sesame oil
400ml (14fl oz) can coconut milk
lime wedges, to serve

Put pork in a shallow non-metallic dish.
Place half the coriander, the garlic, ginger,
3cm (1¼in) lemon grass, lime rind, and
remaining ingredients except coconut milk
in a blender and process finely. Scrape over
pork and stir pork to coat thoroughly. Cover
and refrigerate overnight. Remove pork
from marinade; thread 2 cubes of pork on
each wooden cocktail stick (toothpick).
Reserve marinade.

Preheat grill (broiler). Grill (broil) pork
nuggets for 4-5 minutes a side, brushing
occasionally with some of the marinade.
Meanwhile, scrape remaining marinade into
a frying pan (skillet), add coconut milk and
remaining lemon grass. Boil briskly until
thick. Discard lemon grass. Chop remaining
coriander (cilantro) and add to sauce with
any remaining marinade. Serve hot with
pork, accompanied by lime wedges.

Makes about 30

—— PORK & MANGO SATAY ——

450g (1lb) lean pork, cut into bite-size cubes
2 tablespoons soy sauce
2 teaspoons sesame oil
1 teaspoon each ground cumin, coriander, cardamom
   and grated fresh root ginger
2 ripe mangoes, peeled and pitted
SATAY SAUCE
1 small onion, very finely chopped
2 cloves garlic, crushed
2½ teaspoons grated fresh root ginger
1 teaspoon very finely chopped lemon grass
50g (2oz) creamed coconut, chopped
4 tablespoons crunchy peanut butter

Put pork in a bowl. Mix together soy sauce, sesame oil and spices. Stir into pork. Cover and marinate for at least 4 hours, stirring occasionally. To make sauce, in a saucepan, slowly bring all the ingredients plus 300ml (10fl oz/1¼ cups) water to a boil, stirring until coconut dissolves. Add more water if necessary. Keep sauce warm.

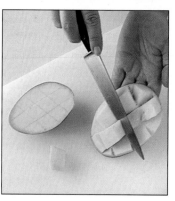

Preheat grill (broiler). Cut mangoes into same size pieces as pork. Remove pork from marinade and thread a cube each of pork and mango on to small skewers. Grill (broil) for about 10 minutes, turning halfway through. Serve pork and mango skewers with hot sauce in a bowl.

Makes about 25

CHINESE BEEF

5cm (2in) piece fresh root ginger, grated
6 star anise
7-8 tablespoons dark soy sauce
150ml (5fl oz/⅔ cup) rice wine or dry sherry
225g (8oz) fillet steak
3 shallots, finely chopped
1 clove garlic, finely crushed
3 tablespoons sesame oil
225g (8oz) red plums, pitted and chopped
5 tablespoons sweet sherry
lime juice and Tabasco sauce, to taste
350g (12oz) small new potatoes, in 2cm (¾in) slices
fresh coriander (cilantro), to garnish

Mix together half the ginger, the star anise, 4 tablespoons soy sauce and rice wine or sherry. Pour over beef, cover and marinate for 8 hours, turning beef occasionally. Cook shallots and garlic in 1 tablespoon sesame oil until soft but not coloured. Add plums, remaining ginger, sweet sherry and 3 tablespoons soy sauce. Boil rapidly until syrupy. Add lime juice, Tabasco sauce and additional soy sauce to taste. Purée in a blender, or sieve. Warm through before serving. (Any remaining sauce can be kept covered in a fridge for several days.)

Preheat oven to 220C (425F/Gas 7). Roast beef on top shelf for 25 minutes for rare, 35 minutes for medium. Meanwhile, toss potatoes in remaining sesame oil. Bake on middle shelf for about 45 minutes, or until tender, turning once during cooking. Cool then thinly slice beef. Arrange some beef on each warm potato base. Add a little warm plum sauce, and garnish with coriander (cilantro).

Makes 60

- WALNUT BREAD, HAM & SALSA -

1 loaf walnut bread, cut into 1cm (½in) slices
2 tablespoons olive oil
175g (6oz) ham, cut off the bone into 15 slices
50g (2oz/½ cup) walnuts, lightly toasted and finely
  chopped
fresh parsley or basil, to garnish
SALSA VERDE
3 tablespoons each chopped fresh mint, coriander
  (cilantro) and basil
1 clove garlic, chopped
2 tablespoons Dijon mustard
3 anchovy fillets
1 tablespoon capers
50ml (2fl oz/¼ cup) olive oil
juice of ½ lemon

To make salsa verde, put all the ingredients
into a blender and mix until smooth. Cover
and chill. Preheat grill (broiler). Brush
bread slices with oil. Put under grill (broiler)
for about 1 minute or until lightly toasted.

Place a slice of ham on each piece of toast.
Top with a spoonful of salsa verde then
sprinkle chopped walnuts over. Cut into
smaller pieces, if you like. Garnish with
parsley or basil.

Makes 15-30

—— BEETROOT ROULADE ——

300g (10oz) cooked beetroot (beets)
2 teaspoons grated onion
¾ teaspoon ground cumin
25g (1oz/2 tablespoons) butter, melted
3 eggs, separated
salt and freshly ground black pepper
FILLING
150ml (5fl oz/⅔ cup) crème fraîche or double
  (heavy) cream, lightly whipped
3 tablespoons horseradish relish
about 2 teaspoons lemon juice
about 1 teaspoon sugar

Preheat oven to 190C (375F/Gas 5). Line
and grease a 23x33cm (9x13in) Swiss (jelly)
roll tin (pan). Put beetroot (beets), onion,
cumin, butter, egg yolks and salt and pepper
in a blender and mix to a purée. Whisk egg
whites until stiff peaks form. Stir
2 tablespoons into beetroot (beet) mixture,
then carefully fold in remainder. Spread in
prepared tin (pan) and bake for 15 minutes
or until just set in centre.

Invert on to a sheet of greaseproof (baking)
paper on a wire rack. Carefully remove
lining paper in strips. Cover with a clean tea
(dish) towel until cold. To make filling,
combine all the ingredients, adding lemon
juice and sugar to taste. Cut roulade in half
widthways. Spread filling over each half.
Starting with a long side, roll up each piece
tightly. Trim edges. Using a large, sharp
knife, cut into about 2cm (¾in) slices.

Makes about 30

TOMATO CALZONE

1.5kg (3¼-3½lb) well-flavoured tomatoes, peeled, deseeded and chopped
salt and freshly ground black pepper
2 cloves garlic, crushed
1 tablespoon olive oil
1 quantity risen pizza dough (see page 86)
85g (3oz) fontina, halloumi or goats' cheese, cut into 36 cubes
small handful basil leaves, torn
beaten egg, to glaze

Put tomatoes in a colander, sprinkle salt over and leave to drain.

In a large saucepan, cook garlic in oil for 2-3 minutes. Add tomatoes and cook until thick, stirring frequently. Season with salt and pepper. Set aside until cold. Preheat oven to 220C (425F/Gas 7). Punch down dough. Break into 6 pieces. Halve these pieces then cut each piece into 3 to make 36 pieces. On a lightly floured surface, roll out each piece of dough to an oval 3-5mm (⅛-¼in) thick. Put a heaped teaspoon of tomato mixture on half of each oval. Add a cube of cheese and scatter some basil over.

Fold uncovered half of dough oval over the filling to meet opposite edge. Press edges together then mark with floured fork tines. Cut 2 slashes in top of each calzone and brush with beaten egg to glaze. Bake for 15-20 minutes until brown and crisp around edges.

Makes 36

RATATOUILLE TERRINE

1 plump clove garlic, finely crushed
4 tablespoons oil from jar of sun-dried tomatoes, or
  virgin olive oil
2 teaspoons pesto
6 large plum tomatoes, cored and halved lengthways
salt and freshly ground black pepper
3 large yellow peppers (capsicums), quartered
  lengthways and deseeded
3 large red peppers (capsicums), quartered
  lengthways and deseeded
1 long aubergine (eggplant), thinly sliced lengthways
2 long courgettes (zucchini), thinly sliced lengthways

Preheat oven to 110C (225F/Gas ¼). Mix
garlic with 2 tablespoons of the oil and mix
pesto with remaining oil; set aside. Arrange
tomatoes on a baking sheet in a single layer
and sprinkle with salt. Bake for 4 hours.
Cool. Meanwhile, preheat grill (broiler).
Grill (broil) peppers (capsicums) until skins
char and blister. When cool enough to
handle, peel off skins. Brush pesto oil over
aubergine (eggplant) slices and garlic oil
over courgette (zucchini) slices. Grill (broil)
in batches in single layers until tender and
lightly browned.

Line a 1 litre (35fl oz/4½ cup) terrine with
clear film (plastic wrap) leaving excess to
cover top. Layer vegetables alternately in
terrine, adding salt and pepper between each
layer. Fold excess clear film (plastic wrap)
over vegetables. Put weights on top and chill
for about 8 hours. To serve, remove weights
and top covering. Invert terrine on to a
board. Using a large, sharp knife, cut into
slices, then halve slices. Pierce pieces with
small skewers and arrange on a serving dish.

Makes about 52

BAKED POTATO WEDGES

5 potatoes, unpeeled, each cut into 6 wedges
4 tablespoons lemon juice
4 tablespoons tomato purée (paste)
1 tablespoon ground coriander
2 teaspoons ground cumin
½ teaspoon hot chilli powder (ground chilies)
salt
4 tablespoons groundnut oil
MANGO CHUTNEY DIP
150ml (5fl oz/⅔ cup) Greek-style yogurt
150ml (5fl oz/⅔ cup) mayonnaise
4-5 tablespoons mango chutney
3 tablespoons chopped fresh coriander (cilantro)

Preheat oven to 180C (350F/Gas 4). To make dip, mix yogurt, mayonnaise, chutney and chopped coriander (cilantro) together. Cover until required. Put potatoes in a large bowl. In a smaller bowl, mix together remaining ingredients, except oil. Stir in 4 tablespoons water. Spoon tomato mixture over potatoes and stir to coat thoroughly and evenly.

Add oil to a roasting tin (pan). Put potatoes and any remaining tomato mixture in tin (pan). Stir to coat in oil. Bake for about 25 minutes, or until tender and a rich brown, shaking tin (pan) occasionally. Serve hot accompanied by mango chutney dip.

Makes 30

— CREAMY FENNEL-FILLED PUFFS —

50g (2oz/¼ cup) butter
70g (2½oz/generous ½ cup) plain (all-purpose) flour
2 eggs, lightly beaten
85g (3oz/¾ cup) grated Gruyère cheese
salt and freshly ground black pepper
1-2 tablespoons freshly grated Parmesan cheese
1 small fennel bulb, finely chopped
200g (7oz/scant 1 cup) medium fat soft (cream)
   cheese
lemon juice, to taste

Preheat oven to 200C (400F/Gas 6). Melt
butter with 150ml (5fl oz/⅔ cup) water in a
medium saucepan, then bring quickly to a
boil. Immediately remove from heat and
beat in flour all at once using a wooden
spoon. Return pan to heat and beat for
1 minute, or until mixture comes away from
sides of pan. Off the heat, gradually beat in
eggs, beating well after each addition, until
dough is shiny and drops easily from a lifted
spoon. Beat in Gruyère cheese and salt and
pepper. Spoon into a piping (pastry) bag
fitted with a plain nozzle (tube).

Pipe 20 small blobs on to greased and
dampened baking sheets, spacing them well
apart. Sprinkle with Parmesan. Bake for 20-
30 minutes until risen and golden. Remove
from oven and make a small hole in side of
each puff. Return to oven to dry out. Stir
fennel into soft (cream) cheese with lemon
juice and salt and pepper to taste. Cut a
diagonal slit in each puff, from top towards
base. Fill with fennel mixture. Serve within
30 minutes.

Makes 20

BROAD BEAN FALAFEL

450g (1lb) frozen broad (fava) beans
2 teaspoons coriander seeds
2 teaspoons cumin seeds
2 teaspoons sesame seeds
leaves from 1 large bunch coriander (cilantro)
leaves from 1 bunch flat-leaf parsley
1 red onion, chopped
2 cloves garlic, crushed
3 eggs
salt and freshly ground black pepper
flour for dusting
vegetable oil for deep-frying
DIP
175ml (6fl oz/¾ cup) Greek-style yogurt
3 tablespoons chopped fresh coriander (cilantro)

Boil beans until tender. Drain well and put in a blender. Heat a small, dry pan, add seeds and fry for 2-3 minutes until fragrant. Add to beans, with herbs, red onion and garlic. Purée bean mixture, adding eggs one at a time, to make a smooth paste. Season with salt and pepper. Chill for 45 minutes.

To make dip, stir together yogurt, coriander (cilantro) and salt and pepper. Cover and chill. With floured hands, shape tablespoons of bean mixture into balls, then flatten them slightly. Heat oil in a deep pan to 180C (350F). Deep-fry balls until crisp and brown, turning once. Drain on paper towels and keep warm. Serve with dip.

Makes about 16

MUSHROOMS EN CROÛTE

115g (4oz/½ cup) garlic and herb soft cheese
20 even-sized mushrooms, stalks removed
8 sheets of filo pastry
85g (3oz/⅓ cup) butter, melted
salt and freshly ground black pepper
1 egg, beaten

Preheat oven to 200C (400F/Gas 6). Divide cheese among cavities in mushrooms.

Brush 4 filo sheets with melted butter. Cover with remaining sheets. Brush with melted butter again. Cut filo sheets into 20 squares.

Put a mushroom, cheese side up, in centre of each square. Season with salt and pepper. Lift sides of pastry over mushrooms to resemble small sacks and pinch neck edges together to seal. Place on a greased baking sheet and brush with beaten egg. Bake for about 15 minutes until pastry is crisp and golden. Serve hot.

Makes 20

BAKED NEW POTATOES

1.5kg (3¼-3½lb) small new potatoes, unpeeled
4 tablespoons soy sauce
2 tablespoons peanut oil
2 tablespoons sesame oil
4 tablespoons lemon juice
25g (1oz) sesame seeds
225g (8oz/1 cup) mayonnaise
grated rind and juice of 1 lime
2 teaspoons grated fresh root ginger
2 tablespoons chopped fresh coriander (cilantro)
finely chopped green part of spring onions
　(scallions), to garnish

Preheat oven to 200C (400F/Gas 6). In a saucepan of boiling, salted water, cook potatoes for 5 minutes. Drain well. Put in a roasting tin (pan). Trickle soy sauce, oils and lemon juice over and stir together. Sprinkle with sesame seeds. Bake for about 45 minutes or until tender.

In a bowl, mix together mayonnaise, lime rind and juice, ginger and coriander (cilantro). Halve the potatoes lengthways. With a melon baller or teaspoon, scoop out a hollow in each potato half. Fill with mayonnaise mixture. Serve garnished with finely chopped spring onions (scallions).

Makes about 28

AUBERGINE BASKETS

2 large aubergines (eggplants)
3 cloves garlic, crushed
1½ tablespoons lime juice
2 teaspoons ground cumin
3 tablespoon chopped fresh coriander (cilantro)
3 tablespoons olive oil
8 sun-dried tomatoes, drained and chopped
16 pitted black olives, finely chopped
freshly ground black pepper
1 packet mini poppadums, about 40
coriander (cilantro) sprigs, and paprika (optional), to
  garnish

Preheat oven to 200C (400F/Gas 6). Cut several slits in aubergines (eggplants) then bake for about 1 hour or until very soft. Allow to cool. Cut aubergines (eggplants) open, scoop out flesh and wrap in a clean cloth. Squeeze hard to remove moisture.

Put aubergine (eggplant) flesh in a bowl and mash well with garlic, lime juice, cumin and coriander (cilantro). Stir in olive oil, sun-dried tomatoes and olives. Season with black pepper. Cover and leave until required. Spoon into the poppadums and garnish with coriander (cilantro) sprigs, and paprika, if using.

Makes 40

COURGETTE DROPS

3 small courgettes (zucchini), total weight 350g
  (12oz), grated
olive oil for frying
1 small onion, grated
1 clove garlic, finely crushed (optional)
small bunch of fresh parsley, finely chopped
salt and freshly ground black pepper
3 eggs, beaten
TOPPING
1 avocado, pitted
115g (4oz/½ cup) soft (cream) cheese
2 spring onions (scallions), very finely chopped
grated rind and juice of 1 lime
1½ tablespoons chopped fresh mint
mint leaves, or finely diced red pepper (capsicum), to
  garnish

To make topping, mash ingredients
together. Season to taste with salt and
pepper. Cover and chill for 1-2 hours. Add
courgettes (zucchini) to a large pan of
boiling water, return to the boil then drain
well. Dry thoroughly on paper towels. Heat
a little oil in a frying pan (skillet), and fry
onion until soft and golden. Add garlic, if
using, and fry for 2-3 minutes. Drain on
paper towels. Mix courgettes (zucchini),
onion mixture, parsley and salt and pepper
with eggs.

Heat a little oil in a large, heavy frying pan
(skillet). Drop large teaspoonfuls of mixture
into oil and fry for 2-3 minutes until golden
underneath. Turn over and brown for about
2 minutes. Transfer to paper towels to drain.
Repeat with the remaining mixture. Put
small spoonfuls of topping on each courgette
drop, to serve. Garnish with mint leaves, or
finely diced red pepper (capsicum).

Makes about 40

— VIETNAMESE CORN FRITTERS —

150g (5oz/1¼ cups) plain (all-purpose) flour
1 teaspoon baking powder
2 eggs, beaten
2 tablespoons soy sauce
2 tablespoons lime juice
grated rind of 2 limes
2 tablespoons chopped fresh coriander (cilantro)
300g (10oz/1¾ cup) frozen corn kernels, thawed
vegetable oil for deep frying
about 32 chicory (Belgian endive) leaves, to serve
coriander (cilantro) leaves, to garnish
SAUCE
4 tablespoons white wine vinegar
4 tablespoons caster (superfine) sugar
1 teaspoon dried chilli (chili) flakes
salt and freshly ground black pepper

In a bowl, beat together flour, baking powder, eggs, soy sauce and lime juice and rind. Stir in coriander (cilantro) and corn. Set aside. To make sauce, in a small saucepan, gently heat vinegar, sugar, chilli (chili) flakes, salt and pepper and 2 tablespoons water until sugar dissolves. Bring to a boil, then remove from heat and let cool.

In a deep, wide saucepan, heat 5cm (2in) depth of oil until a cube of bread crisps in 30 seconds. Add spoonfuls of corn mixture in batches and fry for 2-3 minutes. Drain on paper towels. Put a warm fritter in each chicory (Belgian endive) leaf and spear with a cocktail stick (toothpick). Trickle a little sauce over and garnish with coriander (cilantro) leaves.

Makes about 32

VEGETABLE CRISPS

1.5kg (3¼-3½lb) mixed vegetables such as parsnips,
 celeriac (celery root), sweet potato, kohlrabi, raw
 beetroot (beets), peeled
vegetable oil for deep frying
sea salt
paprika, freshly grated Parmesan cheese, or chilli
 powder (ground chilies) for sprinkling

Using a potato peeler, slice vegetables very
thinly, keeping different types separate.
Keep completely covered in cold water until
required. Drain and dry thoroughly with
paper towels.

Heat some oil in a deep-fryer to 180C
(350F). Fry vegetable ribbons in small
batches until crisp and golden, turning
occasionally. Drain on paper towels.

Sprinkle with salt and flavourings of your
choice. Repeat with remaining vegetables.
Pile into baskets or bowls to serve.

Makes about 1kg (2lb)

MUSHROOM ROLLS

5 tablespoons sesame oil
4 shallots, finely chopped
1 plump clove garlic, crushed
4 teaspoons grated fresh root ginger
450g (1lb) shiitake mushrooms, coarsely chopped
2 teaspoons five-spice powder
salt and freshly ground black pepper
24 sheets filo pastry
sunflower oil for brushing

In a frying pan (skillet), heat oil. Add shallots and garlic and fry for 2-3 minutes. Stir in ginger and mushrooms and cook for about 5 minutes, until tender. Add five-spice powder and salt and pepper. Allow to cool.

Preheat oven to 220C (425F/Gas 7). Brush 1 filo sheet with sunflower oil. Spoon a little of the mushroom mixture near a short edge and roll up, folding in the edges. Place on a baking sheet. Repeat with remaining pastry and filling. Brush with oil and bake for 15 minutes or until crisp. Serve warm.

Makes 24

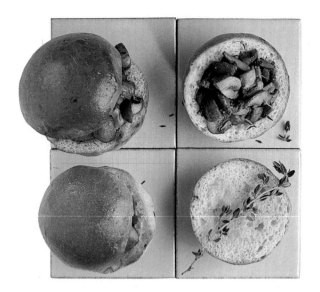

MUSHROOM BRIOCHE

40g (1½oz/3 tablespoons) butter
1 clove garlic, crushed
300g (10oz) brown cap mushrooms, or small wild
   mushrooms, coarsely chopped
1 teaspoon Dijon mustard
2 teaspoons thyme leaves
salt and freshly ground black pepper
20 mini brioches

In a large frying pan (skillet), heat butter. Add garlic and mushrooms and cook, stirring occasionally, for 4-5 minutes, or until tender. Stir in mustard, thyme and salt and pepper. Let cool.

Preheat oven to 180C (350F/Gas 4). Cut tops off brioches, reserving lids. Using a melon baller or teaspoon, scoop out insides of each brioche, taking care not to pierce sides and base. (Use insides for breadcrumbs.)

Place brioches on a baking sheet. Spoon in mushroom mixture and replace lids. Cover loosely with foil and put in oven for 6-7 minutes. Serve warm.

Makes 20

SAVOURY SQUARES

350g (12oz/3 cups) strong (bread) flour
1½ teaspoons easy blend (fast rising) yeast
2 tablespoons chopped mixed fresh herbs
salt and freshly ground black pepper
1 tablespoon olive oil
2 tablespoons red pesto
50g (2oz) thinly sliced prosciutto
150g (5oz) mozzarella cheese, grated
2 tablespoons pitted black olives, chopped
1 egg yolk, beaten with 1 tablespoon water
coarse sea salt for sprinkling

In a large bowl, stir together flour, yeast, herbs and salt and pepper. Add oil and 200ml (7fl oz/scant 1 cup) water and mix to a soft dough. Turn on to a lightly floured surface and knead for about 10 minutes, or until smooth and elastic. Roll out half the dough to line a greased 23x33cm (9x13in) Swiss (jelly) roll tin (pan). Spread with red pesto and cover with prosciutto slices.

Scatter mozzarella and then olives over. Brush edges of dough lightly with beaten egg. Roll out remaining dough to cover filling. Press edges lightly together. Brush top with beaten egg and sprinkle coarse salt over. Leave for about 30 minutes, or until puffy. Preheat oven to 220C (425F/Gas 7). Bake for 20-25 minutes until browned and crisp. Leave to cool in tin (pan) for 5 minutes, then cut into 5 strips lengthways and 10 strips crossways. Serve warm.

Makes 50

RÖSTI

50g (2oz/¼ cup) butter
225g (8oz) onion, finely chopped
450g (1lb) potatoes, grated, soaked in cold water
4 eggs, beaten
3 tablespoons chopped fresh parsley or coriander
   (cilantro)
salt and freshly ground black pepper
olive oil for frying
175g (6oz/¾ cup) soft goats' cheese
3 tablespoons soured (sour) cream
parsley or coriander (cilantro) sprigs, to garnish

Heat the butter in a frying pan (skillet). Add onion and fry for about 5 minutes, or until soft. Drain potatoes and dry thoroughly. Put into a bowl. Mix with eggs, onion, parsley or coriander (cilantro) and salt and pepper. In a large, heavy-based frying pan (skillet), heat oil.

Fry teaspoonfuls of potato mixture in batches for 2-3 minutes on each side or until golden and crisp. Drain on paper towels. Keep in a cool place until required. Beat together goats' cheese, soured (sour) cream and salt and pepper. Cover and chill. To serve, preheat oven to 200C (400F/Gas 6). Put rösti on baking sheets, cover loosely with foil and warm through for about 4 minutes. Top with cheese mixture. Garnish with herb sprigs and serve.

Makes about 60

GRISSINI

450g (1lb/4 cups) strong (bread) flour
1 sachet easy blend (fast rising) yeast
2 tablespoons oil from jar of sun-dried tomatoes in
   oil, or virgin olive oil
300ml (10fl oz/1¼ cups) warm water
virgin olive oil for greasing
6 tablespoons chopped fresh basil
8 tablespoons roughly chopped black olives
DIP
3 large red peppers (capsicums), halved and deseeded
5 cloves garlic, unpeeled
200g (7oz/scant 1 cup) reduced-fat soft cheese
½ teaspoon hot pepper sauce
salt and freshly ground black pepper

.To make dip, preheat grill (broiler). Grill
(broil) peppers (capsicums) until skins are
charred and blistered, and garlic until soft
and charred. When cool enough to handle,
peel off skins. Purée peppers and garlic with
cheese and salt and pepper in a blender.
Cover and refrigerate for at least 2 hours.
Stir flour, salt and pepper and yeast
together. Stir in oil and water and beat to a
soft but not sticky dough. Knead for about
10 minutes until smooth and elastic. Put
into an oiled bowl. Turn to coat with oil,
cover and leave until doubled in volume.

Preheat oven to 200C (400F/Gas 6). Halve
dough. On a lightly floured surface, knead
basil into one half and olives into other
half. Divide each piece into 16. Roll out
pieces in turn to pencil shapes about 23cm
(9in) long. Transfer to baking sheets. Bake
for 15-20 minutes, or until golden and crisp.
Remove to a wire rack to cool. Serve with
the dip.

Makes 32

MINI PIZZAS

450g (1lb/4 cups) strong (bread) flour, plus extra for
   dusting
1 sachet easy blend (fast rising) yeast
salt and freshly ground black pepper
200ml (7fl oz/scant 1 cup) warm water
2 tablespoons virgin olive oil, plus extra for brushing
virgin olive oil for greasing
TOPPING
2 tablespoons virgin olive oil
2 shallots, finely chopped
2 cloves garlic, finely crushed
450g (1lb) mixed brown, shiitake and oyster
   mushrooms, diced
1 tablespoon chopped fresh tarragon
250g (9oz) jar hollandaise sauce

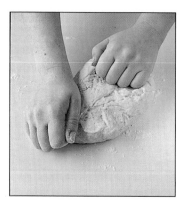

In a large mixing bowl, stir together flour,
yeast and salt and pepper. Gradually stir in
warm water and oil and beat to a soft but
not wet dough. Turn on to a lightly floured
surface and knead for 10 minutes, until
smooth and elastic.

Put into an oiled bowl, cover with clear film
(plastic wrap) and leave until doubled in
volume.

To make topping, heat oil in a frying pan (skillet), add shallots and cook until tender and lightly browned. Stir in garlic and mushrooms and cook for a further 5 minutes or until all the liquid has evaporated. Add tarragon, and salt and pepper to taste. Set aside.

Preheat oven to 230C (450F/Gas 8). Oil 2 baking sheets. Punch down dough and knead briefly. Divide into 16 pieces. Roll each piece to 5mm (¼in) thick circle.

Transfer dough circles to baking sheets. Brush with virgin olive oil. Spoon on mushroom mixture. Bake for about 10 minutes or until bases are crisp and browned. Preheat grill (broiler). Spoon hollandaise sauce on to pizzas and put briefly under grill (broiler) until glazed.

Makes 16

MEXICAN MINI MUFFINS

175g (6oz/¾ cup) butter, softened
175g (6oz/¾ cup) cream cheese
2 small eggs
115g (4oz/1 cup) each self-raising flour and cornmeal
pinch of baking powder
salt and freshly ground black pepper
1 red pepper (capsicum), deseeded and finely chopped
GUACAMOLE
3 large avocados, pitted
1 clove garlic, finely crushed
1½ tablespoons finely chopped red onion
¼ teaspoon ground cumin
pinch of chilli powder (ground chilies)
juice of 1 lime
3 tablespoons chopped fresh coriander (cilantro)
1 large tomato, deseeded and finely chopped

Preheat oven to 180C (350F/Gas 4). Grease 40 mini muffin tins (pans). Beat butter and cheese together then beat in eggs. Mix flour, cornmeal, baking powder and salt and pepper together then gradually stir into butter mixture. Add red pepper (capsicum). Spoon into tins (pans) and bake for 20 minutes or until golden.

Meanwhile, make guacamole. Mash avocados with garlic, red onion, spices and lime juice. Stir in coriander (cilantro) and tomato. Season to taste with salt and pepper. Serve muffins warm, accompanied by a bowl of guacamole.

Makes about 40

———— ORANGE TRUFFLE CUPS ————

250g (9oz) plain (dark) chocolate, grated
1 egg yolk
1 tablespoon unsalted butter
1 tablespoon finely grated orange rind
100ml (3½fl oz/scant ½ cup) whipping (heavy)
  cream, whipped
fine strips peel from marmalade, to decorate

Put half the chocolate into a heatproof bowl over a saucepan of hot water. Stir occasionally until chocolate has melted.

Using a small pastry brush or paint brush, brush melted chocolate over inside of paper petit-four cases. Leave to set then repeat and leave until firm. Make a small tear in paper case then carefully peel off.

Meanwhile, in a heatproof bowl over a pan of hot water, warm remaining chocolate until almost melted. Add egg yolk and stir until thickened. Remove bowl from heat and stir in butter and orange rind. Set aside to cool to room temperature. Fold in cream and spoon into a piping (pastry) bag fitted with a star nozzle (tube). Pipe filling neatly into each chocolate case. Decorate with peel from marmalade.

Makes 24

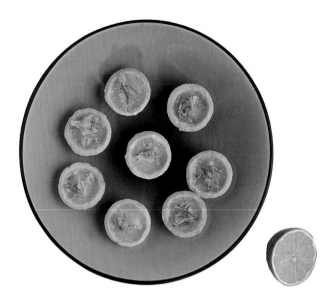

LIME TARTLETS

175g (6oz/1½ cups) plain (all-purpose) flour
85g (3oz/¾ cup) ground almonds
2 tablespoons caster (superfine) sugar
115g (4oz/½ cup) butter, diced
1 egg yolk
FILLING
4 eggs
115g (4oz/½ cup) caster (superfine) sugar
2 tablespoons crème fraîche or soured (sour) cream
150ml (5fl oz/⅔ cup) lime juice
DECORATION
thinly pared rind of lime
2½ tablespoons caster (superfine) sugar

Stir flour, ground almonds and sugar together in a bowl. Rub in butter until mixture resembles fine breadcrumbs. Add egg yolk and 1-2 tablespoons cold water and mix to a dough. Knead briefly, cover and chill.

Put dough on a lightly floured surface. Cover with baking parchment. Roll in one direction to 5mm (¼in) thick.

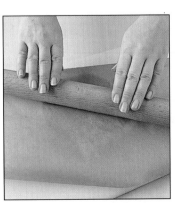

Preheat oven to 190C (375F/Gas 5). Cut out rounds using a 5cm (2in) cutter; gently press into tartlet tins (pans). Lightly prick bottom of shells. Chill for 30 minutes. Bake for 10 minutes. Cool. (Leave oven on.)

To make filling, whisk together eggs and sugar. Stir in crème fraîche or soured (sour) cream and lime juice until evenly combined. Pour into tartlet cases. Bake for 15 minutes, or until filling is set. Serve warm or cold.

To make decoration, cut lemon rind into short, fine strips. Blanch for 2 minutes in boiling water. Drain. In a small pan, gently heat sugar in 2 tablespoons water until dissolved. Add lime strips and simmer for 8-10 minutes until strips are transparent and water has evaporated. Remove strips with a slotted spoon. Decorate tops of tarts before serving.

Makes 24

NUT & COFFEE MERINGUES

2 egg whites
115g (4oz/½ cup) caster (superfine) sugar
50g (2oz/½ cup) ground walnuts
chocolate-coated coffee beans, and pecan halves,
   to decorate
FILLING
about 200ml (7fl oz/scant 1 cup) double (heavy)
   cream
about 1 tablespoon icing (confectioners') sugar, sifted
about 1 teaspoon espresso coffee powder

Preheat oven to 120C (250F/Gas ½). Cover baking sheets with baking parchment. Whisk egg whites until stiff. Gradually add sugar, whisking constantly, and continue to whisk until mixture is very stiff and shiny. Gently fold in ground walnuts. Spoon into a piping (pastry) bag fitted with a plain nozzle (tube) and pipe about 45 small discs of meringue on the baking sheets. Bake for about 1 hour until dry, very lightly coloured and can be lifted easily from baking parchment. Cool on a wire rack.

To make filling, whip cream with sugar and coffee to taste. Just before serving, pipe a small swirl of cream on each base. Decorate some with chocolate-coated coffee beans and some with pecan halves. Serve in small paper cases.

Makes about 45

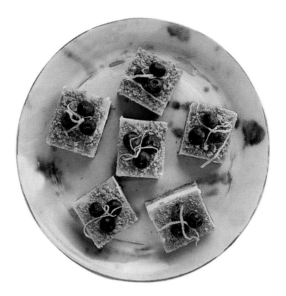

CHEESECAKE SQUARES

85g (3oz/⅓ cup) butter, diced
150g (5oz/1¼ cups) self-raising (self-rising) flour
50g (2oz) amaretti biscuits, finely crushed
50g (2oz/¼ cup) plus 1 tablespoon caster
  (superfine) sugar
1 egg yolk plus 2 eggs, separated
225g (8oz/1 cup) mascarpone cheese
225g (8oz/1 cup) ricotta cheese
1 tablespoon cornflour (cornstarch)
grated rind of 1 lemon
1 tablespoon rum
50g (2oz) amaretti biscuits, in coarse crumbs
raspberries, blueberries or sliced strawberries, to
  decorate

Preheat oven to 200C (400F/Gas 6). Grease
and base-line a shallow 20cm (8in) square
cake tin (pan). Rub butter into flour until
mixture resembles fine breadcrumbs. Stir in
finely crushed amaretti and 1 tablespoon
caster (superfine) sugar. Mix to a dough
with 1 egg yolk, plus a little water if
necessary. Knead lightly. With finger-tips,
press dough into base of tin (pan). Cover
with foil and top with raw rice or baking
beans. Bake for 10 minutes.

To make filling, beat cheeses together then
mix in remaining caster (superfine) sugar,
egg yolks, cornflour (cornstarch), lemon rind
and rum. Whisk egg whites until stiff then
carefully fold into cheese mixture. Pour on
to pastry base. Sprinkle amaretti crumbs over
top and bake just below centre of oven for
1¼ hours until just firm in centre. Leave to
cool in oven with heat turned off. Cut into
small squares. Decorate each square with a
raspberry, blueberry or a strawberry slice.

Makes about 64

— SPICED HOT FRUIT KEBABS —

1kg (2¼lb) prepared mixed fresh fruits such as
  mango, papaya, pineapple, nectarine, plum, banana,
  lychees, cherries
150g (5oz/⅔ cup) unsalted butter
3 tablespoons grated fresh root ginger
1 tablespoon icing (confectioners') sugar
1 tablespoon lime juice

Soak about 20 bamboo skewers in water for
30 minutes. Cut fruit into bite-size chunks.
Thread a selection of fruits on each skewer.

Melt butter and stir in ginger, icing
(confectioners') sugar and lime juice.

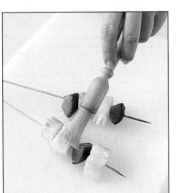

Brush over kebabs. Preheat grill (broiler).
Cook kebabs, turning frequently and
brushing with butter mixture, for about
5 minutes until beginning to caramelize.
Serve warm.

Makes about 20

— CHOCOLATE MINI MUFFINS —

150g (5oz/1¼ cups) self-raising (self-rising) flour
2½ tablespoons cocoa powder
1 teaspoon baking powder
pinch of salt
50g (2oz/¼ cup) light brown sugar
1 small egg, lightly beaten
150ml (5fl oz/⅔ cup) milk
50g (2oz/¼ cup) butter, melted and cooled slightly
½ teaspoon vanilla essence (extract)
chocolate and hazelnut spread or chocolate frosting,
 for filling

Preheat oven to 200C (400F/Gas 6). Grease 20 mini muffin cups, about 4.5x0.5cm (1¾x¼in), or put small paper cases in cups.

Sift flour, cocoa powder, baking powder and salt into a shallow bowl. Stir in sugar. Stir egg into milk, butter and vanilla essence (extract). Pour on to dry ingredients and mix briefly using a large metal spoon and a lifting figure-of-eight movement; there should not be any free flour but mixture should still be lumpy.

One third- to half-fill paper cases or muffin tins with mixture. Put ½-1 teaspoon of spread or frosting on each portion of mixture and cover with more mixture so that cases or cups are almost filled. Bake for 20 minutes until risen and tops spring back when lightly touched. Paper cases can be removed immediately, alternatively place cups on a wire rack and leave to cool for 5 minutes, then remove muffins from cups. Serve warm.

Makes about 20

INDEX